Published by Ice House Books

Copyright © 2019 Ice House Books

Written by Moira Butterfield
Illustrated by Pedro Demetriou
Designed by Emily Curtis

Ice House Books is an imprint of Half Moon Bay Limited
The Ice House, 124 Walcot Street, Bath, BA1 5BG
www.icehousebooks.co.uk

ISBN 978-1-912867-11-0

Printed in China

WHEN YOU'RE IN LOVE WITH A VAMPIRE...

ICE HOUSE BOOKS

WHEN YOU MEET A VAMPIRE

HOW WILL YOU KNOW IF YOU MEET A VAMPIRE?

Here's a handy checklist to run through.
If your new friend fits them all, you can
be pretty sure their fangs aren't fake.

1. Vampires **DON'T LIKE DAYLIGHT**, though club DJs and teenagers don't either, so delay whipping out the stake and hammer until you're absolutely sure you're dealing with the undead.

2. Vampires are on a strictly-protein diet of **BLOOD**. Definitely no carbs or veg. Offer them a doughnut or a carrot stick and check out their reaction.

3. Vampires flinch at anything religious. **HUM A HYMN** and watch closely to see if they twitch.

4. Vampires have obvious, not to say 'pointed', dental issues. Does your new friend have **UNUSUALLY LONG FANGS?**

5. Vampires tend to stare at necks as if they're looking at a delicious plate of chips. If they ask for a bite, **GET READY TO FIGHT.**

WHEN YOU MEET A VAMPIRE

VAMPIRES GIVE THEMSELVES AWAY BY ROCKING A SUPER-COOL STYLE LOOK. HERE ARE SOME VAMPIRE CAPSULE WARDROBES.

WOMENSWEAR

SLINKY SUPERMODEL
- Black body-con maxi
- Glamorous neck-grabbing gloves
- Hair straighteners (female vamps like long hair but not curls, which are too princess-y and not undead-y enough)

STEAMPUNK WENCH
- Victorian outfit
- Black bead choker (to hide bites)
- Super-red lipstick (to hide blood)

MENSWEAR

GOTHIC JAMES BOND
- Tuxedo evening wear
- Opera cloak
- Hair gel (male vampires love a hairdo)

STEAMPUNK TRAVELLER
- Victorian outfit
- Top hat
- Coffin accessory (it's a portable bed)

WHEN YOU NEED TO VAMPIRE-PROOF YOUR HOME

NO VAMPIRES

- ARE YOU WORRIED ABOUT VAMPIRE VISITS?

- VAMPIRE-PROOF YOUR HOUSE IF YOU THINK THE LOCAL BAT-BOYS AND GIRLS ARE TARGETING YOU AS A BLOOD-DONOR.

DON'T PUT OUT THE BAT MAT
They say vampires can't cross thresholds unless invited, so don't ask them in.

DECORATE WITH GARLIC
Vampires famously hate garlic so hang lots of it everywhere. Your house will stink and you'll never get visitors.

Add surprise garlic home accessories your vampire attackers won't expect, such as garlic toothpaste and garlic toilet cleaner.

LIGHT UP THE NIGHT
Vampires are allergic to the ultra-violet light in sunlight, so get some UV lighting. It won't burn them to ash like a sunray, but it might make them crispy enough to think twice about fang-jumping the host.

WHEN YOU NEED TO VAMPIRE-PROOF YOUR HOME

Old legends tell us that **VAMPIRES ARE OBSESSED WITH COUNTING** and one way to delay them is to put a fishing net outside the door. They have to stop to count the holes, apparently, giving you time to get out your hammer/stake combo kit.

VAMPIRES CAN TURN INTO ANIMALS – not just bats, but rats, owls, moths, foxes and wolves. So if you live in a vampire hot-spot don't go out wildlife-watching in your garden after dark and don't let anything fang-y through your cat flap (apart from your cat).

DRAC-BAT

RAT-BAT

VAMP-WOLF

FEATHERY FANG-OWL

HAIRY NECK-SUCKER MOTH

FANGY-FOX

WHEN VAMPIRES MOVE INTO YOUR NEIGHBOURHOOD

SPOT THE SIGNS THAT YOUR 'HOOD MAY HAVE AN INFESTATION OF VAMPIRES.

People are dressed for Halloween every day of the year.

Nobody eats the garlic bread at your barbecue.

Your neighbour mows his lawn at midnight, in full evening wear.

The tanning salon and the sunglasses store shut but somebody opens a cloak shop and a Blood Bank Café.

All the car plates are from Transylvania.

VAMPS ARE IN THE 'HOOD!

WHEN YOU NEED TO FIGHT OFF A VAMPIRE

A VAMPIRE IS A FORMIDABLE FOE, BUT IF YOU GO FOR ITS WEAK POINTS YOU STAND A CHANCE OF STOPPING THAT SUCKER.

START WITH THE HEART
The vampire's weak point is its heart. Aim for it with a sharp blade.

GET HOLY
Vampires hate holy water and crucifixes, both of which will freak them out long enough for you to overcome them.

FINISH THE JOB
Bladed weapons are useful for decapitating the undead, but be sure to follow up with a staking and burn the remains of your vanquished vampire. It's best to be on the safe side.

LET IN THE SUN
The sun will finish off a vampire, so time any confrontation at sunrise and suddenly pull the curtains/blinds back with a flourish...Ouch!*

*Check the weather forecast in your area before mounting an early morning raid on a vampire. Dense cloud could lead to awkwardness.

NEED TO FIGHT OFF A VAMPIRE

HERE ARE SOME MORE VAMPIRE KILLING SUGGESTIONS FROM OLD MYTHS AND RECENT MOVIES.

Scatter some mustard seeds. The vampire will stop to count them, giving you the chance to stake the maths-obsessed bat-geek from behind.

Trap the vampire in the cross-shaped shadow of a windmill, should there be a handy one locally.

Get a cockerel to crow.

Throw peppermint at the vampire.

Stick an iron needle (or better still, a sword)
into the fang-fiend's heart.

Throw the vampire into freezing water.

WHEN YOU WANT TO USE AN ANTI-VAMPIRE STAKE

FOLLOW THIS STEP-BY-STEP GUIDE TO SUCCESSFUL VAMPIRE STAKING.

I Use a wooden stake, preferably cut from a hawthorn or rowan tree.

II Thrust firmly at the heart on the vampire's left side. Not your left side. Their left side. Mixing it up would be a rookie error, and your last as a living human.

III

Burn the dead vampire and bury it at a crossroads, face-down, so it gets really confused if it wakes up and tries to rise. **JOB'S A GOOD'UN**

WHEN YOU WANT TO BE A VAMPIRE HUNTER

WOULD YOU LIKE A CAREER AS A VAMPIRE HUNTER, BUFFY-STYLE? HERE'S WHERE TO LOOK FOR OUR BLOOD-SUCKING BUDDIES.

WHITBY, UK
Dracula landed here in the novel by Bram Stoker. It's become a big hang-out for Goths. Could some of those black-clad eyeliner-addicts be real vampires?

NEW ORLEANS, USA
According to the bestselling novels of Anne Rice, this southern city is a vampire hotspot. Look out for them trying to blend in with the crowd at Mardi Gras time.

TRANSYLVANIA, ROMANIA
Vampires 101. The classic Vampire homeland. There are enough old castles, weird villages and lonely mountains for them all.

US HIGH SCHOOLS
There's a lot of high school vampire action in TV shows and movies, but don't worry. Buffy, the greatest vampire slayer of them all, has it covered.

WHEN YOU NEED TO DISGUISE YOURSELF AS A VAMPIRE

IF YOU'RE WORRIED ALL YOUR FRIENDS AND NEIGHBOURS ARE VAMPIRES YOU MIGHT WANT TO BLEND IN. IT'S NOT JUST A CASE OF FALSE FANGS...

DO A VAMPIRE LAUGH
Mwahahahahahaha.
Note the mwa and the large ha count.

DO THE STARE
Watch any old vamp movie and you'll see the villains staring down their victims, trying to hypnotise them with googly eyes.

WORK THE CLOAK
Old-school vampires are always flicking their cloak out. It's probably a comfort habit, like thumb-sucking (but vampires suck other people's thumbs).

WHEN YOU THINK YOU MIGHT BE DATING A VAMPIRE

YOUR DATE IS A VAMPIRE IN DISGUISE WHEN:

They have deadly-pale skin and dark circles round bloodshot eyes, but they are not a student.

When a bat flies by, they say "Hi Dad".

Their latest holiday trip was a night flight to Transylvania to 'hang with the family'.

WHEN YOU'RE IN LOVE WITH A VAMPIRE

OH DEAR. SO YOU'VE FALLEN BIG-TIME FOR A VAMPIRE. WELL, THEY ARE KILLINGLY ATTRACTIVE. HERE ARE SOME TIPS FOR GETTING ALONG.

You'll need to persuade your loved one to stay off the blood. Try replacing it with another highly-addictive food such as chocolate, ice cream or those little cocktail sausages that nobody can stop eating at parties.

Wear a polo neck at all times to discourage love bites.

Carry an emergency garlic clove for those moments when your vampire goes batty.

Clip your loved one's wings so they don't fly off with some other vamp.

Buy your beloved an electric toothbrush for those awkward teeth cavities.

WHEN YOU NEED TO BREAK UP WITH A VAMPIRE

SO IT'S 'FANGS FOR THE MEMORY', HUH?
HERE'S HOW TO UNHOOK FROM YOUR UNDEAD BOYFRIEND OR GIRLFRIEND.

BREAK THEIR HEART
Literally. The stake is a brutal technique, only to be used if your partner has really upset you by nibbling someone new or gone back to their antisocial blood-sucking ways.

THE HUMANE WAY TO GIVE YOUR BAT THE PUSH
Try saying one of the following and your unwanted vampire will probably disappear before your eyes.

WHEN YOU MARRY A VAMPIRE

ARE YOU THINKING ABOUT SPENDING THE REST OF YOUR LIFE (AND POSSIBLY YOUR AFTERLIFE) WITH YOUR BELOVED BITER? HERE ARE SOME DOWNSIDES, BUT IF YOU STILL WANT TO GET MARRIED AFTER YOU'VE READ THIS, GOOD LUCK! HAVE A FANG-TASTIC WEDDING!

Many married couples have to get used to their partner snoring but you will have to get used to sleeping in a coffin.

Your in-laws could be tough to get along with, but expect visits because vampire families are close-knit (blood is thicker than water).

If you have kids together, they may have extra-fussy food issues. That, and they might turn into bats.

Expect judgmental comments: "Don't you even have a cloak?" and boasting: "Of course, we are frequent flyers". But be nice to them. Anyone's relatives can be deadly dull, but yours are deadly.

WHEN YOU ARE COOKING FOR A VAMPIRE

IF YOU'VE DECIDED TO BE FRIENDS WITH THE VAMPIRES IN YOUR LIFE YOU MIGHT WANT TO COOK THEM A MEAL. HERE ARE SOME DISHES THEY COULD GET THEIR TEETH INTO. WARNING: VEGETARIANS AND VEGANS, LOOK AWAY NOW.

BLACK PUDDING
Pig's blood mixed with fat and oatmeal to create a delicious sausage. This and other blood sausages are available in many countries around Europe.

BLOOD PANCAKES
A Scandinavian treat of milk, flour, egg and pig's or cow's blood.

BLOOD CURD
Congealed and dried animal blood is used as a thickener in Asian sauces and stews. In Korea it's considered a hangover cure.
Is getting drunk worth **THAT?**

BLOOD SOUP
Prepared in many cultures. In Poland you might be offered czernina, made of duck blood with stock and possibly some noodles if you're lucky.

WHEN YOU WANT TO REMODEL YOUR VAMPIRE HOME

MOVED IN WITH A VAMPIRE? TRY THESE PRACTICAL IDEAS FOR MAKING YOUR HOME MORE VAMPIRE-FRIENDLY.

ADD MORE HANGING SPACE
Bats will appreciate spacious sleeping areas.

BLOCK UP THE WINDOWS
For your overall lighting design, take inspiration from the kind of shadowy underground nightclub where the DJ looks suspiciously like the undead.

TAKE OUT MIRRORS
Vampires have no reflection. Use the space you gain for a cloak rack and hat stand.

BECOME SPIDER-FRIENDLY
Never vacuum up the cobwebs again. Let them drape, haunted castle style.

WHEN YOUR BESTIES ARE VAMPIRES

HAVE FUN WITH YOUR BESTIE VAMPIRE FRIENDS SO THEY DON'T BECOME A PAIN-IN-THE-NECK.

Take your vampire friend to a vampire movie. Here are some suggestions:

DRACULA
Old-school Dracula tales will remind your friend of family videos.

TWILIGHT
Soppy sexy love stuff with added blood-sucking. Will they love in vein?

INTERVIEW WITH A VAMPIRE
A-Listers Tom Cruise and Brad Pitt wear fake fangs and get their teeth into vampire roles.

Take up hang-gliding so you can have some great nights out together.

Avoid bestie sleepovers or wear garlic-impregnated pyjamas.

WHEN YOUR BESTIES ARE VAMPIRES

5 THOUGHTFUL THINGS TO DO FOR YOUR VAMPIRE FRIEND.

1. Give your friend breath-freshener lozenges. Vamps have evil breath.

2. Never 'out' your vampire bestie on social media. Buffy is bound to have a Google Alert set up.

VAMPGRAM

JEFF91
Hanging with ma boi &lit

3. If your fang-friend is doing their best to give up blood, don't take them to a meat counter. It'd be like taking a vegan to a hog roast.

4. Praise your friend for their retro look (nobody has worn cloaks like that since the 1800s).

5. Mark your vampire friend's birthday but remember that vamps live forever unless hunted down, so you'll be making a big commitment.

WHEN YOU WANT TO MAKE A VAMPIRE LAUGH

MAYBE YOU COULD DELAY A VAMPIRE ATTACK WITH ONE OF THESE JOKES, THOUGH TO BE HONEST THEY REALLY SUCK.

I knew a vampire who became a poet. He went from bad to verse.

Why do vampires take cold medicine? For their coffin.

What do you get if you cross a vampire with a snowman? *Frostbite.*
Why did the vampire break up with her boyfriend? *He wasn't her (blood) type.*
Why are vampires like false teeth? *They come out at night.*

TRY NOT TO UPSET A VAMPIRE UNNECESSARILY WITH COMMENTS LIKE THESE.

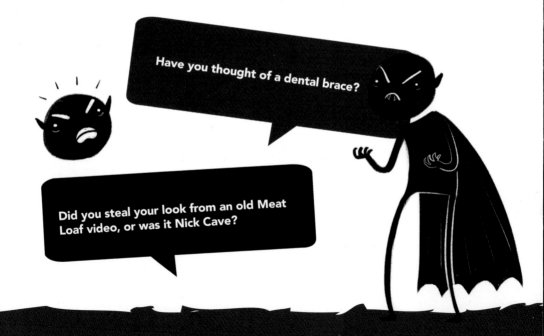

WHEN YOU MEET A VAMPIRE ON HOLIDAY

VAMPIRES BEHAVE DIFFERENTLY AROUND THE WORLD. HERE IS A VAMPIRE GUIDE FOR GLOBETROTTERS.

SOUTH RUSSIA – A Russian legend says that people who talk to themselves are at risk of turning into a vampire. It might be best not to mutter in the street if you want to avoid stares, and possibly stakes.

MADAGASCAR – Vampires are said to eat nail-clippings as well as blood on this African island. Expect to see them lurking near nail bars.

TRANSYLVANIA – A Transylvanian vampire is an evil spirit who has possessed a corpse. It's a batty body-snatcher. No wonder it's allergic to religion.

WHEN YOU MEET DRACULA – CELEB BLOODSUCKER

DRACULA IS IN THE BUILDING!
(DID YOU LEAVE A WINDOW OPEN?)

THERE ARE AT LEAST 10 THINGS YOU NEED TO KNOW ABOUT THE LORD OF THE NIGHT WITH THE A-LIST BITE.

1. He was introduced to the world in Bram Stoker's novel, written in 1897. It kicked off modern vampire folklore with its charming but deadly coffin-kipping villain.

ALBANIA – A vampire witch called a shtriga is said to live here. She turns into a flying insect. Has she not heard of fly swats?

CATALONIA – An evil vampire dog called Dip is said to live in these parts. He should really change his name to Fang.

HUNGARY – Hungarian vampires are said to obsessively hoard treasure. Mess with their stash of bat bling at your peril.

IRELAND – Fairy vampires are said to live here. They're not cute. They're cutthroat.

GREECE – Greek legend says you can become a vampire if a cat jumps over your grave, which seems a bit random and very unfair to our furry friends. They only have little fangs, after all.

2. He likes the ladieees, and he's always looking for a new bride.

Dracula-tastic chat-up lines:
"Shall we go for a bite?"
"If I said you had a beautiful corpse, would you hold it against me?"

3. He's said to be based on Transylvanian nobleman Vlad the Impaler, a violent monster who terrorized people in the 1400s. Vlad is said to be related to UK top royal Prince Charles. Just saying.

4. Dracula's bark is not worse than his bite.

5. He has a castle on the edge of a steep precipice. All its doors are creaky.

6. In Bram Stoker's novel, Dracula trained at an evil version of Hogwarts called Scholomance. The pupils didn't do tests. They did blood tests.

7. Drac-ie is on an extreme diet regime. Blood only. No gluten. Only globin.

BLOOD

8. He can change the weather, causing storms and thunder. This is a very useful skill for film soundtracks.

9. He can only sleep in sacred Transylvanian earth, which he keeps in his coffin as a sort of scratchy batty comfort blanket.

10. He has a long list of jokes. What's his favourite coffee? De-coffin-ated. What's his favourite ice cream? Vein-illa. And so on.

WHEN YOU GET BITTEN BY A VAMPIRE

IS IT ALL BAD IF YOU GET BITTEN AND BECOME A VAMPIRE YOURSELF? LOOK ON THE BRIGHT-SORRY-DARK SIDE. THERE ARE UPSIDES.

JEFF'S REAL DEAL

You won't have to watch daytime TV ever again.

You get to wear a cool cloak and you can rock a top hat if you want to. Nobody will laugh (and live).

You'll never have to change the duvet cover again because you'll be sleeping in a coffin from now on.

You won't have to go to an overpriced restaurant and pay loads for wine. Just drink from the waiter.

You will fit right in at a Goth Convention without having to spend any money on eyeliner or silly boots.

WHEN YOU GET BITTEN BY A VAMPIRE

HERE ARE SOME PROBLEMS YOU MIGHT ENCOUNTER AS A NEWLY-BITTEN VAMPIRE.

I'M A VEGAN
Try to wean yourself off blood, as you once weaned yourself off bacon and sausages. Unfortunately vampires don't like lentils because they have no pulses. Mwahahahahahaha!

I DON'T LOOK GOOD IN BLACK
You could go for a purple or deep scarlet costume, though you may find you do suit black once your skin turns a deathly pale.

I HAVE A LOT OF DAYTIME HOBBIES
Take up new sun-free hobbies such as star-gazing or moth-collecting. Haunting can be a lot of fun, too. Look for an undead club in your area.

I'VE ALWAYS BEEN SCARED OF BATS.
I hate them fluttering near me... You'll find you're cured of your phobia and you can hang with the bat crowd in any convenient cave or castle dungeon. Enjoy!

WHEN YOU ARE A VAMPIRE BUT YOU WANT TO TURN HUMAN

IS THERE A CURE FOR A LIFE OF NECK-GNAWING? NOBODY KNOWS FOR SURE, BUT HERE ARE SOME LEADS.

Historians think that diseases such as rabies may have spawned vampire myths. You could ask your doctor for rabies shots, and perhaps some cream for that coffin rash.

Genetic DNA medicine might work.
Or it might not. Your bite.

If you can stay off the human blood for seven years you can stop being a vampire, though when you die for real you will probably become a vampire again. Sorry.

Eating the ash of a burnt vampire may do the trick. That sounds like the worst barbecue food **EVER.**

DRAC

×

WHEN YOU LOOK LIKE A VAMPIRE BUT YOU AREN'T ONE

DO YOU LOOK SO KNACKERED THAT PEOPLE MISTAKE YOU FOR THE BLOOD-SUCKING UNDEAD?

Stop wearing so much black, get more sleep and start eating healthily or risk meeting someone who's read this book and has a handy stake…

Hey, fangs for reading! Sleep tight tonight, and don't let the big bats bite!
You'll find you're cured of your phobia and you can hang with the bat crowd in any convenient cave or castle dungeon. Enjoy!